Prophecies From My Heart

ARSENIO SORRELL

This is a work of fiction. Name places, characters and incidents are the product of the author's imagination or are used fictitiously. Any resemblances to actual persons, living or dead, events or locals is entirely coincidental.
Copyright © 2023 Arsenio Sorrell
All rights reserved. No part of this book may be used or reproduced in any manner without the written permission of the copyright owner except for the use of quotations in a book review.
First paperback edition March 2023
Book design by Arsenio Sorrell
Cover design by Caterina Sauro
Edited by Valerie Lorraine Productions
All rights reserved.
ISBN: 979-8-9850841-6-0
ISBN: 979-8-9850841-6-0

Published by
Lulu.com

Dedication

This book is solely dedicated to Lolita, my mother.

She transitioned from this world June 16th, 2020, after a short battle with Covid. It was at the beginning of the pandemic and was by far the worst year of my life. We had just begun a reset on our relationship together and it is the most painful thing I've ever experienced.

After being able to cope a bit, I vowed to continue her life and legacy living on. My mother was always most proud of my acting and writing talents more than the others. I chose writing and since then I've begun the journey with her watching as my ancestor, my guardian angel.

Thank you mom for everything you've ever done for me and how you continue to show up even in your physical absence. I love you more than anything in this world!

"For I know the plans I have for you," declares the Lord, "plans to prosper you and not to harm you, plans to give you hope and a future."
Jeremiah 29:11

About The Author

Arsenio Sorrell is an artist, actor and healthcare professional from Wisconsin. As a family man who enjoys the scenic atmosphere of his home state, he exchanges time out of a busy lifestyle for time with nature and wildlife to help inspire his writing. He also finds inspiration from literally everything he is around and exposed to. He hopes to reach a vast amount of people and impact their lives heavily. After accomplishing many things he plans to leave society to spend the rest of his life in the Mountains.

Known on his social media as Deep Thought The Lyricist, Arsenio has a popular following for his work. He considers himself a 'lyrical connoisseur' which is probably the reason his writing is so strong. He is the 2 time Floetry Poetry Sensual Slam Champion, the Purple Poetry Slam Finalist, an Improv Poetry 24 Hour Prompt Slam Finalist, and a member of the Deadly Pens poetry collective. Arsenio has also been featured on platforms virtually and performs for in-person events in several states across the U.S.

As Arsenio continues to work on his craft, turning it into a profession, he has taken his most personal and meaningful of his pieces and created his first book, Prophecies From The Heart. This removes 'aspiring author' from his list of goals and adds Author to his artistic resume. You can find Arsenio on Instagram @deepthought_thelyricist and on Clubhouse at Deep Thought The Lyricist to enjoy more of his intensely great works. He can also be booked for in person or virtual events at Wordzmcgee@gmail.com

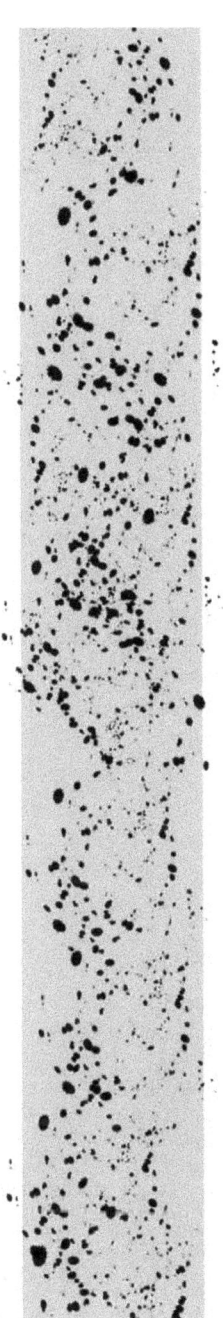

TABLE OF CONTENTS

MAMA	9
A GIFT JUST FOR YOU	11
A MAN IS NOT SUPPOSED TO CRY	13
CITY SOULS	15
MALE ROLE MODELS	20
E. HOLLINS	23
FIREWORKS AND GUNSHOTS	25
DISTANCE	28
SLIPPERY WHEN WET	32
MAMAS TEARS	35
FORGOTTEN CHILD	38
GENIE IN A BOTTLE	40
QUESTIONS IN MY HEAD	42
AWAY AWAY	45
SO FAR GONE	47
MAKE IT ON MY OWN	49
WHAT ARE YOU HERE FOR	51
PLATINUM	53
SINNERS	58

PROPHECIES FROM MY HEART

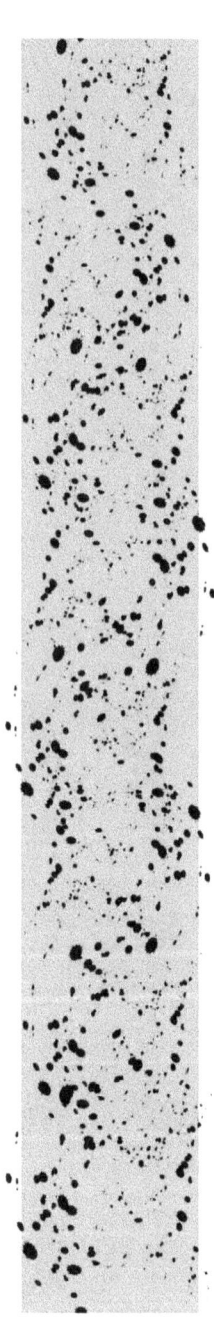

TABLE OF CONTENTS

TATTOO INK ARMS WITH NARCOTICS	61
HOLD YOUR HEAD	65
AMBROSIA EYES	68
HEARTKBREAK SONG	71
MAYBE IT'S JUST ME	73
FRUIT BASKETS	76
FUNERALFOOD	79
FAMILY IS THICKER THAN BLOOD	81
BALLAD OF A NOBODY	84
WAR WOUNDS	86
TIRED OF RUNNING	88
SUPERMAN	89
THIS IS WHY I WRITE	92
EVERYTHING IS MADE UP	95
POETRY TEARS	99
A NEW FAITH	103
MY FIRST BIRTHDAY	106
PROPHECIES OF THE HEART	110

PROPHECIES FROM MY HEART

Dear Mama

Dear Mama,

Things are a little different now, within an instant how could we have ever made it here, with me on the ground and you somewhere in heaven up above the clouds. I remember as a child seeing you cry and not having a clue why, or what to do so I cried too. I've never been in a Tsunami but mamas tears always seemed to drown out everything else. It's common to mimic your parents as you grow, so your trials and tribulations were the potters hands that molded me. Today I'm seeing you like I never have before, and it's hard to speak with this knot in my throat, but that same knot ties in so many things instilled in me that you had a way of bringing it out. No matter what, I can do all things through Christ who strengthens me. That base was set to build the foundation that I stand on to this day. Mama I understand everything you said in your testimony to me that one morning, and I learned to accept you for who you are. It was unfair of us to ever have criticized and try to change you, see because god makes it very clear that he wants us to give and love unconditionally. You did that through

Prophecies From My Heart

everything people threw at you, stood strong and accepted them back without question. So the times you were jumped on, lied to, cussed out, betrayed, disrespected, or people just flat out forgetting that superheroes need solace too. As for me? Well, I apologize for being a part of that group at times, I didn't understand then...but things have been clarified. So I can see clearly now because mamas tears have dried up and she's safe in God's arms. So please don't be afraid mama and know that we will take care of each other like we should have been doing all these years, I love you and I can't wait to see you again someday...

Love,
Your Baby Boy

A Gift Just For You

...I made you this macaroni necklace,
You see, it's common to gift parents with things that we make in school as a kid
and I made you this macaroni necklace, my teacher says your mom or dad will love this so make sure to make it special
I painted mine with the colors of love because let's be honest...
Macaroni should look like a Valentine since so many people love it
my teacher says to make sure to also write them a letter to let them know you love them
We will surprise your parents by placing it in your locker and your parent will get it when they pick you up
Well, if the teacher says it then it must be true so this necklace, I have is just for you
and I conjured up all my truth to write this letter,
it reads:

Dear Dad

I love you.
This macaroni necklace is for you, and it's painted with my love.
    Love,
Your Son.

Prophecies From My Heart

I let the paint from the necklace drip on to my letter
hoping it would have some flare
my teacher saw it and wiped it off thinking it was an
accident and now there's a smear on my letter
but there's still color so it should mean a lot
but now the letter reads:

Dear Dad,

I miss you.
This macaroni necklace is for you and is painted,
with my sadness.
    Love,
Your Afterthought

My macaroni necklace sat in my locker the rest of the
school year with my letter until the janitor tossed it
away to keep infestations away
My father never came back then and has been mostly
gone ever since
but if he ever wanted his macaroni necklace
I'd make him one and re-write the letter and put
them together like glue

here dad I got a gift...just for you

A Man Is Not Supposed To Cry

Be solid; never let them see you **crying**
Crying unfolds indications of **weakness**
Weakness is for women and women **only**
Only now Men stare face to face with a world owned by
them
Them, men who follow an unwritten law that ruling is a
divine purpose for **guys**
Guys, all guys who are pressured into an **image**
Image of what a Man is, and isn't supposed to do
Do as you please as long as you never illustrate **failure**
Failure to evolve into that CEO, Athlete, famous actor
lawyer, doctor, rock star, **Rapper**
Rapper with no quality lyrics just songs **dissing women**
Dissing women to boost confidence, and **self-esteem as a**
Man
Self-esteem as a man comes from others downfall
Downfall from godly to **human**
Human because nobody attains the life of **perfection**
Perfection is the largest figure to **stand next to**
Stand next to your young self and tell me they wouldn't be
ashamed of you
Ashamed of you for suppressing **your fears**
Your fears pushed to the back of your mind right next to
tears
Tears and sadness are for gay men and women to **express**
Express to me what the difference is **between us**
Between us...I know a gay man is still **a Man**
A man with responsibilities goals and openly conveyed
fears

Prophecies From My Heart

Fears that give them reason to **verbalize emotions**
Verbalize emotions that should be declared **shamelessly**
Shamelessly doesn't mean publicly, it means **trust**
Trust that you put in the hands of **another**
Another time goes by where you degrade a man due to his likes or **sexual preference**
Sexual preference is his **personal life**
Personal life of yours that makes you believe you have the right to **belittle a man**
Belittle a man by saying he is not a man, in a **disrespectful manner**
Manners are made for boys, who grow up to control their **household**
Household that is ruled by abuse, fear, and **inadequate communication**
Inadequate communication between Dad and **family**
Family who unknowingly carries the **tradition**
Tradition that says a man isn't still a man if he **cries**
Truth be told, a man is only a real man if he not only can but **does cry...**

City Souls

I can hear the city breathe in its sleep
creep from alley ways in between buildings
Renaissance echoing trumpet horns, notes float like respirations
I'm one with the streetlights standing on the corners like dope boys
We were on fire once upon a time and simmered to coals to cook up immaturity
Purely these ideals surely kept us captivated
burned out from the street fights and my knuckles been bleeding but that won't stop me from trying to recreate the building blocks
Laying cement and the red bricks
Our foundation was placed in boundaries set by older brothers, uncles, absentee ballot fathers
The mother's that thrived but were only fed with temporary comfort like menthols
That smoke engulfed us, so we didn't see what was outside the community
We remained with those who were willing to be present

Prophecies From My Heart

hoping they fit well enough to piece
together the village that it takes to
raise children
The bandages and ointment to mend
us together for the healing
That gate I was placed up against
and patted down despite not fitting
descriptions
Conflicted because I felt they were
"just doing their jobs"
but my best friend's father was
filled with fury that vented air that
would consume fumes although he
was ignored
It sat with me for years like the man
at the bus stop divided into
proportions
His life escorted into mental illness
forced
and little did we know it reflected
on us
So, we're feeling less beautiful
because their colors are distorted
visions extorted because innocence
is attractive in any form and we
were always shaped differently
through this molding
I walked the street on my birthday
one time pouring my heart out to
my best friend
he told me the story of how his
father had passed away

he used to drive city buses, but his real drive was in his children
His mode of transportation was his honesty and commitment
Vivid how his smile would spread across the world like sunrise on horizons
I grieved his passing because good fathers should live forever
dead-beats should let the beat drop
5-part harmony from graffiti, hair salons, corner stores, park benches and the tears of abandoned children
I'll let that marinate a little because it's too seasoned to bypass reason
It was all natural and grief is the meat of food for thought...so mentally I became vegan
I've funnelled anger into the streets because it ripples heat waves into our lives
Embodied the feeling of pride feeling so alive so we start to climb
to see if there was enough distance in between the curbs to show me which way I should go
the suburbs were always just for show and for us down here that's where the sidewalk ends

Prophecies From My Heart

right after the barbershop where
life breathes through clippers
cutting through the bullshit
sometimes I like to lay in the
middle of the street at night and
pretend I can control the narrative
headlights expose my
vulnerabilities because the city
was good to me
but my heart resides in the
mountains
I'll always love the city though
because it's in my soul
Dripping down from gutters into
the sewers that are the pits of my
spirit
Twisted in the fingers of shake ups
between gangs that were initially
formed to protect the
neighborhood
Now they're the downfall and
primary captor of city souls
The bus rolls by picking up
grandma to usher her to church
Bible clutched in one arm and
handbag in the other
The roaches crawling through her
house waiting for remnants of
Sunday dinners

The city controls you,
holds true to enclosed
dreams and we were told
too
There's no way outside of
sports, rapping and pure
luck
I didn't just used to love
her, she's my stronghold,
so I speak into her ear I'll
always love you...

Male Role Models

The men I grew up around can be described as dope boys, hustlers, boss type niggas
killin bottles of Remy, henny, gin and all the shit gangsta rap told us what "real niggas" do
I remember being told during exchanges that I didn't see what just happened
my best friend saying school wasn't for him so he dropped out
my cousins going off to the other room and locking the door
and the aroma of weed filling the house where the kids played
but you can't take days off in the street
so, in the night they just smoke and drink till their minds fade
they taught me that it's every man for themselves, be tough
Take down as many women as you can
dope rides and fly clothes, speeding down the road
see I thought I was cool when I was with them
even though they limited what I could do
and before shit got too real, they'd drop me off
see the men in my family always showed glimpses of compassion
a hint of support to let you know they still there but that fast track kept them from consistency
my lil cousins soaking it all up and wantin money

so, them circling around to make that runback was
a roundabout that connected chain links to the
youngins
who longed to know what it's like to smoke that
weed
and make exchanges for change but not the right
kind so they only ended up being rich with issues
I went to visit my uncle in jail one time, and he told
me he was in there for stupidity
at the time I didn't know what he meant
and now the sands of time would often turn to
quicksand
the older men would grab hold of the younger ones
consequently bringing them down too
we stand on the branches of our family tree
every now and then somebody slips off or gets
pushed, in an attempt to save our own asses
as we fall into a noose of lynching so my family stay
crippling each other like they tryna dodge war
drafts
and I'm past the bullshit because I was that
superstar who they wouldn't let succumb to the
streets...
but I admit I liked to throw hands whenever I had
the chance
Hell...I partially did it to brag to them
but as I fought for acceptance, I realized this
costume I was wearing made me weary early on
and I wouldn't be able to keep up as things got
wilder
so, I became knocked down with fury...without an
outlet
my family thrives off anger and oppression
fucked up toxic relationships and depression
I'm wondering what this tree was ever rooted to,
as I watch another member of the family's wrists
get laced with handcuffs

Prophecies From My Heart

CHEST PUNCH

KNOCKED DOWN

STAND UP

CHEST PUNCH

KNOCK DOWN

NOW STAND THE FUCK UP AND TAKE THAT SHIT LIKE A MAN!

And if you cry, we gon hit you again
I want to step in to show some compassion through this counterproductive ravaging
I have an opinion to express from my young voice but that don't matter in the hierarchy of a black family
we were beat as slaves to keep discipline and order
then we carried those lessons down to our sons and daughters, but I can't tell you why
so, I drop tears and cry hoping the water from my fears will revive this family tree before it's chopped down for wood to make our caskets
because what they're doing destroys life biting wood takes down the tree during a period where the term-mite eat the trunk from under us
then we turn to dust as our generations dive face first into being completely forgotten...

E. Hollins

Dear E,

It's been years since we spoke bro and I've never been quite sure why
It still throws me because we used to be so close
Last time I saw you, you were still in the life you dropped out of school for
That's how you met my oldest brother and he offered to introduce us not knowing you were already family, but the vibe was different
We were both doing what we have to in order to survive in life
You in the streets, me still in school workin a 9-5 on the total opposite tip
Moms used to tell me stories about the road on the path you had chosen
I wanted to visit you in the hospital when ops caught you lackin
Wanted to write you letters in jail when the cops came and snatched him
I heard you got a little one and never received an invite to the shower
When we were young, we swore this world was ours
the day you told me you would drop out of school was the same day where our relationship became what it is at the point of this letter
We will always be family and I'll hold on to that pride
Mama always said hangin around you I would either go to jail or I'd die

Prophecies From My Heart

You already hit one of those street goals
I say goals because other than the fast money it's all you can really look forward to, Speaking of moms, you know she's gone now...
I'm not sure if you heard because you didn't reach out to acknowledge that or otherwise
Anyway, homie I hope you're still alive finding a way to thrive
Hopefully the next time we speak won't be when me and your casket meets.

Love you bro...

Fireworks and Gunshots

Fireworks go pop, gunshots go bang

When I was a kid, we used to go see fireworks
every Fourth of July
the show was cool, but I was only there for the
finale
where they would shoot off rapidly painting the
sky with colored cinders
it seemed like some reached the stars saw an
airplane flying and wondered what it looked
like from their view
doesn't matter because we were too busy
dancing watchin our shadows move like a rave...

Fireworks go pop, gunshots go bang

We was at the park being kids, playin basketball
but I couldn't play well so mostly just watched
my forte was foot races
I was elite...fast as fuck they would say
so when the gunshots at the park went bang I
had no doubt that I would be fine
but these shots were nothing like the ones
outside of aunties house
outside of grandpas house
that one day crept into grandpas house
right before the flash that caught the neighbor
in the back of the head as for grandpa and
grandma...

Fireworks go pop, gunshots go bang

Prophecies From My Heart

Those fireworks probably looked like
flickering solar lights from heaven
levitate the mind into presents
my best friend almost blew his hand off
because it seemed like it was a dud
he put it to his ear and heard it hiss like a
snake which was indication to know
that if he would've thrown it any later then
he would've lost his finger when it exploded
but that's okay he only lost his hearing
temporarily so he had to lay low so he could
hear the close calls

Fireworks go pop, gunshots go bang

One into my cousin,
gunshots go bang
one into her sister,
gunshots go bang
one into her brother,
gunshots go bang
one into aunt in law,
bang into baby cousin then
bang into their grandma,
brother survived only to hear the
gunshot hit him in the chest and take his
breath away years later,
it all felt like a movie,
or show on tv,
no sun no moon,
and he proved that night that blood was
thicker than family because flesh can't stop
the impact of anger that releases souls
quicker than the bullet in the chamber

Fireworks go pop, gunshots go bang

She couldn't tell the difference just knew that one kept her up at night,
the **fireworks** torched my uncles hand and the shit look like Freddy Krueger,
the gunshot took my friend's mind out his thoughts to rest,
brain matters but it's the heart that gets the last laugh,
fireworks out a hole through my Batman blankets before it tore through the screen,
house filled smoke but I made sure that mama didn't smoke me,
because the little that she knew was efficient bout guns and bullets that she told her ex she'd put through him if he ever touched her again,
gunshots shot into the air on my mother's birthday because it was new year,
and I always wondered how many people may have died from the **gunshots** masking each other,
some in the sky some you just wonder, and if I shoot for the stars will they make it just as far as the **fireworks** or will they stop,
maybe the **fireworks go bang** and the **gunshots go pop**,
they take away more **fireworks** shows every year so in the future I know there will be no mix up over what goes **pop** and what goes **bang**...

Distances

The mind plays tricks, portrays
holograms and mirages
if you're not hip to magicians and
illusionists, it's easy to feel the lift
of your soul so impossible to ever
calculate where thoughts go when all
that you know ceases to flow, I'll be
damned...
so, I find myself next to you as you sleep
off the overdose of what we call love
your pulse is the calmest it's been in a
while
It's hard to be angry in REM stages but
that doesn't make the dreams less vivid
Our last memories are often the times
that impact us the most so somehow
I can't even imagine your smile
Your touch doesn't feel the same
those goosebumps reverse because the
sound of your voice makes my blood boil
so, I stay thinkin...wishin that this
toxicity would lie dormant
so maybe for a little while longer we can
have that moment of potential where
other couples envy us,
when you get emotional, I do too
your emotions are confined to
disappointment and sadness
Mine? anger and fear, so you see...we are
no longer equals

Standing on opposite sides of the equation but it's the final solution
so no crossovers could multiply these problems that are infinite
They say sometimes the greatest journey is the distance between two people
And we have ceased to be intimate
so right now, we couldn't be any further apart...
even though I'm right next to you
I wanna hold your hand but my touch alone can't fulfill the promise that we won't end up like this again
we know from past experiences that once you're stuck it's a broken record the cycle keeps repeating

it's a broken record because the lyrics cause the cuts to deepen

it's a broken record because even if we move the needle, we still just go in circles seekin

it's a broken record because let's be honest...this machine has reached its limit a long time ago

but like most bad habits we cling to them like it's an angel come down to bless us
I still think you're beautiful, your scars are beautiful,

Prophecies From My Heart

your eyes are what take me away and my
words brought you close to your funeral
I kiss her on the forehead and do my best
rendition of trying to walk away
hoping she won't come back but I know
she will, so I'll wait
knowing damn well nothings gonna
change but we will keep at it, looking for
a different result...
the definition of insane
and we'll love each other in the worst
way possible until one of us is
completely useless from these mental
and emotional abuses
so, we'll settle for fool's gold because on
the outside it looks the same
We continue to push forward knowing it
never feels as good as the first hit of
blow and you're my drug of choice
I just wish I wasn't the cause for the
hopelessness in your voice
as it fades off into the distances
Menacin the way this pernicious
interaction is pretentious to my pride
consume your knife with my heart
because it's not quite heartbreak so the
feel is different
I've seen this in visions, and she missed
it because she only paid attention to my
potential
so, what else could keep her afloat?

Nothing so if I sink, she'll go
down with me drowning quickly
because this is way too heavy
for her to ever start to
comprehend
and frankly I'm not strong
enough to deal with it either...

Slippery When Wet

Getting a grasp on life...
it's entirely possible to find that your rear end is occupying rock bottom,
A helping hand doesn't help much when they're folded across arms observing,
don't help when they're holding cell phones recording,
and so, my life in the spotlight is the Truman show,
showmanship is given so we can learn appreciation so I'm waitin patiently,
watching my step because I like to practice cadence, but my metronomes broke,
life's slippery when wet and even worse when you can't swallow what it brings and choke,
this knot in my throat is composed of my hope instead of pride,
that won't go down the drain as easily,
I really want your eyes to view my heart, my soul, like really see me,
the way my chakras beam and rainbow rays highlight me as a unicorn in human form
Because I've always been different heading
D
O
W
N
these slopes

Fighter in my soul but every once in a while, I have to hang on these ropes
I'm so doped up on falsehoods sometimes my reality is impaired
So, I'm slippin,
I'm slidin,
it's wet I'm hiding
Froze over and solidified me as bi-polar
Which means my world will always be twice as cold
Not as of yet am I finding,
that the reflection from the puddles I'm cryin, strike me like lightning
It's an anomaly hittin every time in the same spot

Boom! That's what you get, hope now that you understand
Boom! Poke your chest out and show that you're a man
Boom! Another stretch with little to no sleep, What's your plan?
Boom! Drain pill bottles till I can't stand
Boom! Another cut to the arm,
Boom! Another cut to the arm
Boom! Another cut fingers gripping the blade trying to hold on to life

And my journal is covered in blood because those cuts couldn't sever my ties with depression

Prophecies From My Heart

So, I cry from the abandonment as
my little cousin comes into my
room
I'm only conscious enough to tell
her to get the fuck out
Maybe soon enough that the
demons won't get her this time
And I scream as I disintegrate
into cocaine lines
I feel invincible I mean invisible
all the time
Plus, how am I supposed to know
life's slippery when wet if they
don't give any caution signs...?

Mama's Tears

The world was in the process of forming a new history for documentaries, books and pictures worth more than a thousand words
Multiplied by a million-man march happening right outside my car window

And all I could think of was the fact that it might rain
Hoping those raindrops would take the place of mama's teardrops so she wouldn't have to cry anymore
The man I was becoming...
Since we first put this future into motion prepared me
But even in full pads and complete awareness the impact of that hit left me shattered

I took a deep breath before I told her it would be okay hoping it would mask the same fear, I had of what could be
Because no matter how strong you think you are,
Witnessing your mother cry is a thousand heartbreaks
Crushing windowpanes glass stained with all these words you only familiarized with in movies

I couldn't say much until I saw you
Then throat knots threatened to take my breath away

Prophecies From My Heart

And not untangle until I'm strangled
with the pain of seeing you THIS way
For a while now I picked my words
carefully
Because the parallel of poor word
choice and anger are never worth the
deficit

So, I reiterate that I love you
In the midst of a time where hatred
would be clawing its way through
our conversation turned argument
So, what we had built before was
often on unstable foundation

It would fall apart until one day
instead of using the same rubble to
build
we cleared it and made a field
where we planted seeds for love to
grow between us
Reflections of grandma came with
more stories, and I finally
understood

Then I started to miss her...even
though we had never actually met
before
I could feel the lineage following
along my veins spreading like tree
branches
For me this is one of the only times I
felt forever in something so close to
me

It's poetry in motion rhythms flow but as rhythms go there's nothing more impactful than ballads
So, I can't help but think about the tears you would've cried seeing yourself in that condition
Likely knowing that you were leaving soon
Hurt you couldn't comfort everybody here to ease the process

I wonder if you ever cried when you were pregnant with me
I wonder if the tears rolled down your pregnant belly
Absorb through your belly button
Through the umbilical cord and soak into the strands of my DNA
I can still remember seeing you cry when I was a child so naturally I cried too
I witnessed you stop breathing so I pushed out what was in my lungs hoping I would die too

You didn't cry when you died and I'll always wonder why
I know it's god's plan for none of us on earth to survive our human lives
But I'd give my own breath for one more moment with mama instead of her watching over me in the sky...

Forgotten Child

All I can remember are the yesterday's that
present themselves as today
but I wish the gifts were tomorrows
like if Santa Claus gives the bad kids coal
is it still considered a gift?
I used to not give a shit
mostly because of the households I was
birthed from
an absent father...a mother who was there
but goin through the motions
but I had no use for an apparition nor a
hologram...
Where's my solace?
It'd be better if I never obtained
knowledge, abstained logic
like I maintained until I could learn
enough to surpass my blood stains
The stains on my carpet
stains on my journals
stains on the razors that rested under my
pillowcases when I couldn't find anything
to believe in
I tried looking you in the face but there
was always another sibling consuming
your time
always assumed to be okay
How could you not check for sure?
My heart was so pure, I never had the ill
intentions
Self-destructing as often as I could
manage, it trickled into my future
I was forgotten, distraught in this world
that at one point I fought in, postpartum,
anxiety was just a part of him
With my life at stake

I pleaded for you to stay, even
now I hunger for the thirst to
be quenched from your love
Long standing is this drought,
this pain, with whom do I draw
to fill this void?
Will father ever remember
that I'm a part of him?
Will mother ever remember
where she forgot the little boy
so innocent?
Forgotten...

Genie in a Bottle

It was your favorite song
used to play it on repeat
dancin to the lyrics even when you'd eat
it was funny then
you weren't the best at dancing, but you
did a mean 'runnin man'
the smile on your face when we came to
visit was heartwarming
and that's how I remember you best
but those memories turn to fog when I
start to remember the rest
remember you at rest
thinking we're the same age and I never
even had similar thoughts to what you had
never felt the amount of bullying you
experienced inside and outside your home
I told myself I would write about you
someday and to make it creative
but I paint pictures, so I have to make this
vivid,
the details of your death to this day make
me livid
I wish I could've held your wrists
your hands before you broke the skin
tore into your childlike innocence, gaped
the possibility of your future
I wasn't there but I still have visuals of
your lifeless body floating in your own
blood
I embodied that pain, those cuts
my tears flow to this poem as I write
genie in a bottle playing on repeat

I was terrified of you at
your funeral
it was so surreal, but it was
reality
it's too difficult to continue
this piece without breaking
down
and letting my anger get the
best of me
so, I'll leave it at I love you
and I hope you're finally at
peace...

Questions In My Head

Dear mama,
I always thought the people that died before their time were lucky,
to be honest I still do,
Ya know, I still think about that one January 1st where I almost aligned my day of death with your day of birth,
that day was colder than anything going on outside,
My reflections on a countdown of your respirations knowing I could've kept you going,
defy the majority with my selfish intents as the reasoning,
I saw you in some of my patients a couple months after,
the one who couldn't speak and got violent,
the one who couldn't move in bed,
the one that was only brought in to be placed in a nursing care facility as a new base,
because you wouldn't return home in the best of cases,
Was it love or wasting time?
I can't seem to place my finger on it and even if I could, what's the point?
Then my emotions flip to anger, and I drag other people into it mentally wishing I could trade their life for yours,

Because yes, I know that heaven is the ultimate goal but why did it have to be you?
For God's sake I just wanna know so much,
does the heart of God ache because he knows we will be in pain still,
I maintain still because I know,
but the differences they talk about knowing in serenity prayers can't seem to cover anything that masquerades itself so freely,
I guess for me it's just hard to accept the things I'll encounter in the future that you won't be there for,
like finding a woman to settle down with, maybe another grandchild that won't get the privilege of being spoiled by you,
I'm trapped in these conversations feeling like when I was in elementary school and other kids would talk about their dad,
My pulse would calm because that's the effect of a deadbeat and for those moments I was wishing I was dead too,
I feel like I'm suffocating, because I'm still here and there's no you,
So, no it's still not fair in my eyes the people walking this earth that lie,
they should be the ones to continue to lie except in dirt,

Prophecies From My Heart

covered by the top caskets and I know
it's God's job to judge but I'll be damned
if I don't have an opinion,
Hell, to be honest I prolly be damned if I
do,
This seems like a nightmare and like I
wanna talk about it,
but I don't wanna talk about anything,
it's not like me to voluntarily come out
of this shell,
and lately I'm surrounded by these
people who I feel I can't trust,
it's tough to distinguish the real from the
holograms so everything looks a certain
way from a distance but when you get
close enough those truths ghost you in
transparency,
I once was so extroverted but reverted
back because of the lessons put before
me,
help me please mama...

Away, Away

Spending her days with her
eyes drifting in the sidewalk
cracks, sidewalk
cracks as her hopes and dreams
start to leak through
through the pain comes the,
comes the, comes the worst
kind
worst kind of people she could
ever imagine in life
in life damn right she'll
encounter people who don't
like her
like her they don't have an
explanation of what's being
done
done to her like they have no
home training
training to be a boxer the way
they use her as a punching bag
bag her feelings up and put
them in her backpack
backpack by the snack sack
sack like a football, like bags
from potatoes
potatoes from the garden of
Eden
Eden of the original days
days original as they come but
the story stays the same
same the way they push her
around

Prophecies From My Heart

around her is spit and gun
wads, paper balls and all
All and more they would
snap her bra and pull her
hair
Hair her mother never
understood why she
didn't like it
it's like nobody would
understand in any other
way
way other than the way
out, but is that not the
only way?
With nowhere to turn to
she leaves school and
runs away
Away, away, away...

So Far Gone

She said I didn't know what else to do
I felt like I should've let you kill yourself...
I know, a heavy way to start a poem but heavy weights sit on my shoulders, ridin on the sheer fact that I can't bear much internally
Enough of the agony will burn in me and mentally I'm yearning for something different, my all I'm givin in every way livin...just enough for it to count
I take the days by the ounce because being high off life can be dangerous by the pound
So, my fists pound my steering wheel as I'm drivin myself crazy
Yellin and screaming in the car because my voice is muffled from an outside point of view regardless of where I use it
My heart is being taken a few thousand miles away, Across the burned bridges that her mother created
Trying to create a clean slate but that's the wrong type of rock to build a foundation, Cemented my legacy in court papers and memories
This bullshit got me so far gone I'm lookin at earth from another galaxy, Trances on trances dazed stances plantin me in fried soil I can't find nutrients in
I just wanna nod away to my music but can't find a song that perfectly fits the way I'm feelin

Prophecies From My Heart

So, I delve into other
emotions like as long as I can
hurt a little it'll feel the same
I stopped writing poems, so I
didn't have to open up,
I don't like people walkin into
my life because they will only
look around and see what's in
the front, not what's in the
back or the basement
So, I closed that door, and
they holler "let me in" but
they look through the blinds
and see what a mess there is,
then they walk away
I can't say what'll happen in
the future, I can only promise
that I will be there
So far gone from this song, so
far gone from this poem, just
so...far...gone...

Make It On My Own

Mama says you're an adult now you can do what you want
But the look in her eyes said otherwise
Besides, I can tell by the tremble in her voice that it felt kind of odd
That's the reason why we're having this dialogue
I'm a rebel, so arguments have become pointless
Which changes mom's focus because at times she knows the connection is gone or broken
So, the body of our conversation falls joint-less
She knew before but now doesn't understand what life means to me as a man
Because I been raising myself since my late teens
And mom has less authority because financially she is no longer supporting me
Things through her eyes seem misshapen horribly
She doesn't know why I chose to take the dark road
And the stains on my feet are composed of blood and street
I'd rather stay in the kitchen and take the heat
It's all because I learned from you to make sacrifices
To tell the true meaning of what my life is
My life's list is filled with flatlines, Lifeless...
I was born to take chances and even step back as long as there's room for advancement
Speak like my voice has enhancements
I've taught myself to always have the advantage
I refused to be looked at as a savage because of my skin color or ethnicity
Or the swag that I have that holds history of a people who struggle against people with a badge

Prophecies From My Heart

Mama I know you worry about the girls that I pick
Because in your eyes nobody's a perfect fit
I know you couldn't teach me everything a man should
And the few guys who tried to be that dad never could
They never understood and for the most part they were no good
But I learned to respect women more through the mistakes they made
You gave me all the tools I need
I know school is important and knowledge is the key
Don't worry about me not going to church either because I know God and we talk regularly
Trust me mom and just be proud
Believe in me when I say
Dear mama I'm a man now, I wanna make it on my own not a handout
Ya baby boy's gon be fine...

What Are We Here For?

In life we strive to find a purpose, blind to all the hurtin, defined by pain birthing, hate my heart because it's bleeding, hate my skin because it makes my rights uneven, and even if things were level, I wouldn't feel eye to eye with the odds, face to face with my fears like I'm my own worst enemy so I'm starin in the mirror, and I ask
~What am I here for? ~

I hear four people saying I'm here for a purpose, its divine intervention, fruitful beginnings, slightly around the edges roundin them up like I'm careful with the trimmings, but I remember so vivid my life being a mistake, like it wasn't supposed to happen but happened to be my parent's fate, this the shit you waited for ain't it!
~What am I here for? ~

I face forward although I'm goin backwards, with my back towards the past I can make the decisions less brash, penny for my thoughts but I'm only receiving brass, like my worth ain't got a worth and it's worse because I'm cursed by the one man who can see into the future but can't show up in the present, I guess my cup runneth empty, this gun is simply put to my temples to blow lyrics into indents like dimples and where the fuck is my potential?
~What am I here for? ~

Prophecies From My Heart

I look around only to see nothing in a crowd full of noise, maybe I'm just a little too paranoid, I smile when I don't want to so I can feel the joy, take steps into the glory, tip toe around the gory scene they made for me, this poem has nothing to do with my life it's somebody else's story, if you put your ear to the shell casing of a bullet you can hear his future scream

~*What was he here for...?*

Platinum

If these walls could talk, then the
conversations with myself would have
substance like infatuated cocaine rushes
that places me as a needle in fantasy
heroine covered by romantic weeds
love drugged me down this path
DOWN
DOWN
DOWN
to the fork in the road
next to the ravine I followed in these
rivers
so serene
Cathartic cleanse by the riverside reaching
down in the water to connect with the
FINGERPRINTS of my **ANCESTORS**
and I can feel their chains
nothing really has changed except we
painted them platinum and gold

Prophecies From My Heart

but this poem is not about them it
goes much **DEEPER**
like molecular level embezzled
the cost of fame from merely a
name
so that surpasses human
chains of society choke down on
my neck incarcerating my
freedom of speech
So, I don't have anything to speak
of...beat down by stereotypes and
reverse expectations I speak
blood
flood my mouth like basements
My voice booms like the base
when the vase shattered and
tombstone statements rained
funeral sticker tapings, tapered
off by latent statements
invasive trapped me in swarms of
faces or at least the backs of them
where people leach **BEHIND MY BACK**
I mean reach **BEHIND MY BACK**

I mean pour bleach into my spine
and break every single vertebra
till I'm cripped like gang banging
blood comin out of me like gang
bangin
six-point star slangin like the star
of David laced with pagans'ritual
and here I am feelin messed up
like Judas provin that I'm just as
UGLY as they are
So why should I care that black
lives matter, that all lives matter
of women's rights
third world countries and their
diseased fight
I just need to get my rocks off and
topped off so I can **DIE HAPPY**
estranged friends and family
I'm cursed spells like a sorcerer
Tryin to see if the **DEVIL** fights up
here in the snow...as well he does
when he went down to Georgia

Prophecies From My Heart

and it doesn't matter because my
tears are still here clenched in
between my teeth
clutched in between my palms
we fight for now when it's trendy but
then the trend is gone
no, the trend moves on and we're left
with residuals
That we'll never benefit from so we
tuck our melanin in our pants
strap belt through belt loops
and play blind until a bullet goes
through somebody else's son **HEAD,
BACK, HEART**, skull cap, fitted hat
Then that gold and platinum, stupid
fuckin drip won't mean shit, right?
Because none of that makes a
difference here and it's worth even
less in the afterlife
So, **LISTEN** to the Caucasoids when
they say act right, like cellphones
when the screen goes white

Nothing else will be seen until our batteries die when they permanently turn off the light
If we don't stick together, we lose our **VISION**, so fathom that into the fabric of your materialism
And that's **THAT** because staring at ourselves on memorial T-shirts like mirrors is how we're taught to **FACE FACTS**...

Sinners

Dear God,
There's a lot that I need to say but I don't want to,
A lot of doors you've opened that I wouldn't walk through
So, I stand here in silent defiance because I feel unworthy
No lie nothing in this world has seemed to suffice
I've been baptized twice but I still don't like water
My life has been reorganized but I can't seem to restore order
I can't afford borders because my kindness is a transporter
Of suppression, which turns to aggression, and these blessings?
I don't know what I'm supposed to do with them
I find myself losing them I mean screws missing
I'm twisted up and confused with sin, I'm magnetic for punishment
I wish the same pull could bring back my screws again
Loose cannon I exposed myself to gang bangin
And for a while it felt natural, the handshakes, the acceptance
I did whatever I wanted, and nobody asked questions
Nothing formed against them shall prosper until I showed them these hands were weapons
Small so I was underestimated and proved I'm not one for testin
Confessin that I needed anger management, so I felt less like a monster
I saw the world and figured I was a menace with nothing else to offer

So, I self-sabotaged to see if when I bleed
would it resemble what would essentially
expose me as a fraud
It seemed so much easier to not be here
than to reset and accept my life was
fucking worthless
A couple years ago I got baptized
For the first time in a long time I didn't
feel lonely
I dropped tears that poured from the eyes
of others in the audience as they listened
to my testimony
My mother was there which solidifies this
memory as one to never forget
She heard some of the dark things that
plagued my mind for most of my life
I chose to leave some things between us
that day,
I know that's okay, that you're looking out
for what's best for me
Through faith I've lost friends, through
hope and the belief I lost more
I don't think I'll ever shed my skin of
abandonment
It spots my surface like freckles or better
yet like leprosy, it's infecting me in the
form of trust
I don't know who to put it in as I'm
thrust...into the spotlight, forced to adjust
Most people associate darkness with
negativity, evil, bad, hopeless
My skin is dark, there's darkness in my
heart, they both are a reminder of where I
come from
I used to want to forget but now I fight to
remember because you can't appreciate the
light without having been in darkness
I'm surrounded by death lately which
brings sadness and is looked at as dark
We don't realize the point is to serve
purpose then ascend to somewhere better

Prophecies From My Heart

So those of us left here are the unlucky ones because we are susceptible to harm, pain, suffering, struggle darkness
Prone to be filled with negativity until we bust
I still can't believe that while we were...are still sinners Christ died for us
Yet I'm here when I maybe shouldn't have been
Naked thoughts as I bare my soul,
Ready and willing to fulfill my purpose...

Love,
Your Child

Tattoo Ink Arms with Narcotics

I'm not submissive to addiction but I need
to feel good, send this pain into remission,
I miss the pure bliss, enriched is the list of
a hallucinating neurotic,
the substance is exotic, inhale, exhale,
tattoo ink arms with narcotics...

Help jog my memory one more time, one
more time,
tell me why I should hit this one more
time,
I'm already high! Take a couple puffs and
let the smoke latch to the sky,
I feel like I'm in a massage parlor receiving
a happy ending,
like that feeling you have when you step
into a hot bath and the water has allowed
your skin to warm up to it,
that feeling you have when the NyQuil hits
of preparing to watch some Dave
Chappelle,
but no matter how hard you're trying or
how high you're flying,
the memories comeback, now you feel like
dying...

I'm not submissive to addiction but I need
to feel good, send this pain into remission,
I miss the pure bliss, enriched is the list of
a hallucinating neurotic,
the substance is exotic, inhale, exhale,
tattoo ink arms with narcotics...

Gimme another shot like you're running up
the score in basketball,

Prophecies From My Heart

I wanna bask in it all, I feel like a king with a needle in my arm,
cuz with the needle I am calm, and feel invincible, immune to the world at least for those precious moments,
I feel like I'm all knowing, glowing bright showing my true colors or floating like gentle falling snowflakes,
until I land in the white breathe in through the nose until I see the light,
hell, it helps me get to sleep at night, when it's all gone and I'm no longer fucked up or stoned,
I feel like dying... So I search for another hit...

I'm not submissive to addiction but I need to feel good, send this pain into remission,
I miss the pure bliss, enriched is the list of a hallucinating neurotic,
the substance is exotic, inhale, exhale, tattoo ink arms with narcotics...

Ahhh! Sorry I thought I saw a purple leprechaun with his chest strapped up with a bomb,
and it scared the shit out of me,
but he jumped from a rainbow that was wrapped around the clouds,
tie dye colors swirling in the background, everything is enhanced I can see the lines in my hand and my future at a glance is slightly more enlightened than I ever imagined,
I'm in a state of intelligent, thoughtful, tranquility,
I'm on point but everybody appears to be laughing and calling me crazy,
Then realization hits, hallucinations flip and my high starts to slip,

Man, I feel like dying, ain't that a bitch!

I'm not submissive to addiction but I need
to feel good, send this pain into remission,
I miss the pure bliss, enriched is the list of
a hallucinating neurotic,
the substance is exotic, inhale, exhale,
tattoo ink arms with narcotics...

I feel good, got a lot of things to get done,
clean the upstairs, downstairs, bathrooms,
wash walls and clothes,
Then I got to go to my job, go to the bank,
go back home, hit the shower cause I stank,
get dressed, clean the upstairs, downstairs,
bathrooms, wash the walls and clothes,
Then I gotta visit my sister before I go kick
it with my friends,
my kids are gettin on my last damn nerve,
I mean making me sick,
Just give me some money so I can get
another hit and stop feedin me that "I'm
broke" bullshit, we supposed to be family,
we supposed to be friends, ya'll won't help
me well fuck you then!
I'll do anything for that fix, couple minutes
later I get me some and I feel new money
rich,
I been up for 3 days, and I don't want to
come down,
been up for 3 days cause I can't lie down,
and now I'll continue my hunt to get rid of
this feeling, that ain't nothin like the first
experience,
the first experience was a laid-back
intense feeling for a cheap expense,
It truly is something I miss,

Prophecies From My Heart

this piece of glass that I light up and kiss
till I'm all filled with bliss,
maybe if I up the dose that I inject or
smoke,
I'll get the very first hit to the power of
the sixth,
no longer am I sore, and you wouldn't be
either if you tried the shit that I scored,
I think my heart skipped a beat but it's
not even beating anymore,
Instead of coming down from the high,
feeling like I want to die,
I collapse to the floor...life nowhere near
perfect,
they say if you die with your eyes open
then you deserved it,
lookin down on my lifeless body, friends
and family hurtin,
I'm thinkin and askin with that same
passion, Was it worth it?

I'm not submissive to addiction but I
need to feel good, send this pain into
remission,
I miss the pure bliss, enriched is the list
of a hallucinating neurotic,
the substance is exotic, inhale, exhale,
tattoo ink arms with narcotics...

Hold Ya Head

How do we keep the music playing?

I'm goin in circles trying to figure out what's
next for somebody like me
I mean if I put it all on the line then
somebody might see
The dirty laundry that snuck in with the clean
Flow so serene, I'm posted up on the block on
a gangsta lean
Sippin on Hennessy tryna get this green
Me? I'm prolific on any backdrop stage or
screen
Loft up into the sky and then I drop off
I can't remember where this ride started but I
got off
Dwelling in memories like I forgot where to
drop these socks off
Maybe the same place that my ambitionz az a
ridah got me popped off
Stuffed stones you ain't hard...you rock soft

Yes, you got to hold ya head...

I'm caught between two worlds hood and
professional code switching
Those to successional bowed head I can't get
my mind right to focus on this confessional
See my expressions pull from past trauma
I'm cool now but I've had drama, I've had
problems
Please your honor, don't pay attention to
these store items that I stole
Don't pay attention to all these fights so cold
Lay in the street till the nights gone
The broken glass that left a nice hole

Prophecies From My Heart

into my soul and because of my belief has
me on my knees for the umpteenth time
this week

How do we get ahead? (Hold ya head)

Put your hands against the fence young
man and spread your legs please
Hold up let me see your face
I mean you don't match the description but
let me search you just in case
I mean if I have the slightest inkling, I
mean even an iota that you fit something
A description, a suit, a casket, a grave plot
then maybe I'll meet my quota
I think I might be some kind of street
wizard that cast genocidal magic spells
over my own people
Don't worry officer I'll murder him for
you, so you don't need to
Because we know they don't give a fuck
about us
And way too often we don't give a fuck
about us either
The only thing we have to quench each
other's thirst is when we pour out a lil
liquor

Too many young black brothers are dying,
(Yes you got to hold your head)

These slave chains own blacks but not
black owned
It's okay they look drippy wet if we just
bedazzle them and cover them in platinum
and gold
Trapped in the fast lane my heart sold to
disciple, I'm psycho
I may not be six feet, but this heat makes
me tower over anybody like the Eiffel

It might go or I might go it's a
question of who releases first?
Me or the bullets in this gauge

Livin fast, too fast

I don't know if you ever check the
news but I'm in there every day
I know the shit in my past was a sin
but I'm in the paper somewhere not
front page but I'm in
Maybe check classifieds to see what
I'm worth to do you favors
Or check the obituaries to see when I
finally made it to my lord and savior
Tupac said you black, SMILE
It's tough because it's a dark world we
livin in
But hope is right in front of you
This land is right in front of you
Black man is right in front of you
I just wanna live for my four kids
Dad, student, poet, healthcare worker
and I'm just tryin to be me
But ask yourself in brutal honesty
What exactly is it that you see...?

Ambrosia Eyes

Abstract emotions shattered into a million sounds
I dwell in your background, cupcake kisses and droplets of passion
but I've died a thousand years in your ambrosia eyes
out of body I am numb to my life, but your eyes guide me up the stairway to heaven
only to pitfall possess me in souls of hell
hail raining down as I hail the simple sound of the thought
of the mentioning
of the switch in your walk
oh, I sink so far down into you mentally
we feed on each other's flaws and hunger for more
My thirst no longer quenched for your love, but my vulnerabilities forsake me
so, I'm interlaced in the roses on your gravestone because to me you are my beautiful in death
but depth uncovers the surfaces of the glow that you yield
and I sunbathe in the aura from your golden eyes, the girl with golden eyes
and I've seen her before in someone else
yet I still can't come close or touch her
and though I will always love her unconditionally I'll also be her worst decision ever made
till death do us to pieces but sometimes a puzzle looks better in the box so you can stare at the cover and wonder what could be
because what could be stands on the tip of the tongue in potential
cathartic sorcery planted deep into your womb

*deep thoughts are in your temple worshipping
your tomb, we speak words opposite of
affirmations but to whom?
I call you names you throw thangs we swang
each other's emotions like hood slang
then there's the make-up sex, like we ain't
feelin shit else so we make up sex to be more
than just foundation and blush
flushed with the way we face cards in an
attempt to show our hands
because green thumbs and red handed don't
equal Christmas, just grinch-ness and my
interests have since changed
now I'm here basking in thunderstorms
hoping that lightning strikes me because it
might be the motivation, I need to pull her
back into the clouds,
looking for number nine but we are constantly
stuck on 1, stuck on 1
stuck on the odds because we're one upping so
it's hard to stay even
but I'm trapped in her Greek mythology
Athena, feenin for a chance to get in between
her good graces again,
chimera is three ways from the broken
mirrors abstracted memories subtracted from
the veins and arteries tendencies
imagery heard like Greek sirens voiced
violence but it's all a part of the grand scheme
crawling up Mount Olympus trying to get a
taste of that ambrosia,
that sweet golden fruit that's nourishment for
the soul making everything better
she was way wetter then, Aphrodite and she
might be the one, 10 shades of the sun
same feathers as when she used to fly high but
like Icarusher wings melted because things
became too hot for her to get close to*

Prophecies From My Heart

*I saw her silhouette and eyes glowing
in the night sky from the moon
gloom and how could this happen so
soon, feeling like I just met you, how
could I have beset you?
I was entranced by your ambrosia, but
you never stood a chance, so all she
could do is sit and watch until she lay
down
never to rise again because when the
soul dies the heart's not far behind and
the body is too
because I'm sacrificing her life at the
tip of my pride,
consuming her in narcissism and
insecurities until she completely loses
herself in trying to become one with
me, so this separation inside, the one
being that we are means that we are
both barren of life...*

Heartbreak Song

Heartbreak song belt notes through melodic

Chords are struck inside of me and are frequently off hue
I was never ready for you to go strings symphonic
Playing keys on the piano to find which one sounds like you

It's like a plague infected my heart when you spoke of us in past tense

Sittin here leaking into the concrete to see if we can blend
Hence, I can be more solid instead of the liquid I've been since
I can't fend off the attempts to bend typing texts but delete instead of press send

Render me defenceless because hearts break like glass

Prophecies From My Heart

Which just cuts your fingers
if you try to pick it up raw
I'm often falling on my ass
because the worst memories
always last
Is this luck or reversed
blessings? It was definitely
love...I know what I saw

I'm a fiend feenin for the
heat that was your love that
made me soft
But as hot things tend to go,
we had to eventually cool
off...

Maybe It's Just Me

It seems to be easier to let
things go
and then open up when it's too
late
so then you can say you lost a
good thing
or it's just always this way
maybe you lacked faith or
missed the signs
being alone is just a state of
mind that feeds ecstasy to
reality
creating abnormalities, orbiting
the feeling to be monogamous
discredit your friends, family,
and children to say nobody is
ever there
that you're lonely, even those
who believe in god keep this as a
"go to" theme for their life
they just wanna feel loved, I
been there many times so I can
speak on it understandingly
is that what it seems

<u>Or maybe it's just me</u>

I could never shed the
impression that I'm a square
don't drink much and smoke
even less

Prophecies From My Heart

my criminal record, don't have
one, seems like because of
this I'm stereotyped
as far as my love life, "I
thought you were only
interested in white girls"
without even asking
some people even go as far as
to bash me
I've never been the guy to
attract girls based on looks
either
my personality and
intelligence usually makes the
playing field even
minus the fact that they have
to try and get to know me
first
can't lie to an extent these
assumptions hurt but what
can I do?
Nobody cares to look into it
Or maybe it's just me
Blood is thicker than...?
Well these days somewhere
between toilet paper and wet
toilet paper
it's difficult to get an "I love
you" but easier to get a see
ya later
holdin close to the outsiders
seems to be the new thing

can't get a response from a text
or a pick-up they just let the
phone ring
I pray for families based off the
stories I hear
the traditional value has
disappeared
family before all even if you're
liquored up they should all be here
lookin out for you
something it doesn't take many
ounces to do
instead we fight and diss each
other like that'll make our friends
think we're cool
fall in love with trends and go
along with it even when it's not
telling the truth

<u>Or maybe it's just me</u>

Things change, people change, time
stays the same
when you die
what will you have liked your life
to be
I want to be remembered and
known well for eternity...

<u>But maybe that's just me</u>

Fruit Baskets

The first things I saw were fruit baskets
Thinking this would be another night of beautiful life but it soured over a few hours
Sinking into the oblivion of what appearances lie in front of me
The fruit was warm as if it had been sitting there for a while but it was still delectable
The arrangements so edible, but then the night got busy
Swarming with needs and delegation of activities so nothing squarely fell on any one set of shoulder
The best part of the fruit was the chocolate covered apples, sweet yet tangy
...I listened to you cough thinking your being here in the first place meant you weren't well
We spoke and in those moments of me walking out something else walked in after me
And the aftermath was accurately placed beyond human capabilities
"WE NEED TO PUSH EPI..."
I'm counting compressions, trying not to be aggressive but I can hear no breaths in progression
just the breathing of "Did I miss something?" Do something wrong? What happened?
I noticed when I came in there was an orangish fruit that I was hoping was mango, but it was cantaloupe
intubated and the tube not making much of a difference...
Shock delivered
I'm envisioning your family thinking Dad or, Husband's gonna be okay, "observation then we'll see him in the morning,"

From the neck up pale as if the soul had
been far gone from this shell
I threw the warm fruit in the garbage in the
room next to the bathroom
The bathroom...where I lowered myself
after the time of death to pray for what his
family would have to endure
Assured that God, My God and hopefully
our God would protect and guide them
He lay there lifeless as bitter as the warm
honey dew lingering on my taste buds
The juice of the fruit couldn't get past the
knots in my throat
I looked in every time I walked past him or
rather his corpse
I can't seem to distinguish from
disrespectful
I could feel the tears as they walked in
Unable to debrief, I internalized everything
in me, trying to think of what to say to help
his family
HA HELP THEM?!?! As if this were normal
here
I knew there was another fruit basket in
the refrigerator
Had my name on it, and a message telling
me I'm amazing
giving thanks for me doing my job
This one had chocolate covered pineapples
shaped like stars
The sky was ripe with a new angel that
night
I stared at his body, waiting for it to get up
not knowing if it would be a miracle or the
opposite
Closed the curtain, and the next time I saw
that room it looked like aftermath

Prophecies From My Heart

I stayed an extra hour, working and
trying to get that fruit to taste like it
usually would and fill the way my
belly feels
The process is so different than the
result, that night will live with me
forever
...God, I wish there had been mangos
I left my basket for the morning crew
hoping the fruit would taste normal
for them
And the honey dew would once again
take on the sweet nectar it once had...

Funeral Food

Outside of botanical gardens the best flowers you'll see are at weddings and funerals, the latter of which can barely be enjoyed because of the bitter smell of death
 Those flowers don't quite smell the same
It's so so...different, what's worse is that damn funeral food
Not that it's disgusting, it's just that no matter how recently it was made it always seems cold
never quite fills the void in your soul but then again
I guess the digestive tract doesn't come into contact with that
I just really, really wish it could though because it's the same food we eat to commemorate spending time with one another on holidays
and it's either too late to be warm or way too heavy of a meal
 so it hits hard like the stories that you have to listen to while your mind is far from the moment
and those stories won't stop because everybody deals with things in their own way so, it's cleansing for people to put their thoughts outside their own mind and essentially on somebody else's shoulders
I have been sore since June 2020, hell to be honest it's prolly been since May
but a lot of it is numbness so it's hard to tell what I'm feeling
so, for the most part I try to write my feelings because the right to feel them is ripe with healing but no single treatment by itself can fix any problem

so that places us here where we are feeling a different kind of pain
it all hurts one in the same, so I often find myself interlocked with the ghosts of my past
I just always crave answers I won't get and even if I do
how can I ever be satisfied with what I receive?
It's hard to believe better days are on the horizon because I haven't quite lost everything yet, but I'm primed to
We live our lives through fear, and I can't lie sometimes those cold bars of the prison built to keep my mind in comfort
I'm driven by something different, something more profound than grieving processes
mental illness and coping mechanisms to deal with this funeral food
we prefer to consume the smoke of marijuana leaves
and Hennessy as if it's not planting seeds of bitter trees with autumns' colors to fall into winters so cold
but these blues won't let go, so how am I supposed to celebrate life when I'm
surrounded by the deceased, constantly I cease to increase my solace
my peace by pieces but I eat this cold but delicious, still missing something with the seasoning
and this pinch of salt will wake up the flavor but it won't wake me up from this nightmare, so I savor the "it's not fair"
 because life's sweet but can't taste the same when you're not there
so, I often only finish my plate hoping the food will soak up the tears, so I don't cry no more...

Family Is Thicker Than Blood

Blood is thicker than water, family is thicker than blood, and we weren't technically blood, but we are family
Life lessons preach to these truths, I speak to what's true, rake through what's new
My words are taped and then chewed, and I ask you, when have you felt at your loneliest?
My moment at the time lay its burden on me at my grandpa's funeral
I stayed in the back to avoid ingraining in my memory the face and body posing as him
I shed tears heavy, I wasn't ready, it was hard to feel it...maybe because I couldn't keep my hands steady
I denied his passing because it's easier for me to believe that I just don't see him often enough
It was often rough and maybe my thoughts are unjust, I wish instead of fingers of self-blame pointing at me they could've pulled together for hands of prayer
Thrust into the shadows I stood there the whole time gazing towards his casket

Prophecies From My Heart

Trying to see through and into the eyes of my grandma, what it's like having to grieve what is said to be the greatest loss in life
Her companion, lover, and best friend, the man she stood next to for over 40 years
The loss of everything she had still stooped low in her eyes
Watching his children grieve the loss of a great father...a feeling I'll never have
As these moments usually push you closer to your family like we're trying to squeeze too many people in a picture
I felt as if it had distanced me more
I watched a piece of me float down into his grave a few moments before they placed the concrete slab over him
"That's it" he's gone...No coming back now
No more cigar smoke illustrating his stories of the past
Gin and whiskey bottles drained completely of their kickback liquids
The last drops dripping down his face past the scars on his neck

Scars from when some men who felt entitled to his jewelry, broke into his house and slit his throat
Maybe he had died then because nothing was the same since...frequent blinking as if his eyelids were robotic
Maybe he was trying to cry, but fear of recurrence made them dry
The tears for his deceased daughter that pushed diabetes through his leg
Or rather where his leg used to be
I never saw him sleep till I imagined him laying on a hospital bed in a coma
Standing next to my mom viewing him for the last time
I still can't stop my hands from shaking...my eyes from quivering and blinking several times as its sprinkler system kicks in
He always used to listen to the blues and as I walked away from his burial site
I finally realized what he was talking about, Yeah Grandpa...I feel it too...

Ballad Of A Nobody

Trying to surpass this feeling that my potential has withered
I can't escape these snakes
on my life they have slithered
I'm bread to be a different loaf in lonesome it bakes

Every Time I climb this mountain high, my soul collapses
My heart skips paces and its pulse is halted
I'm trapped between time frames old soul transferred like synapses
To God I pray hoping to gain an overflow of blessings from the most exalted

It's awfully difficult to keep the depressive animalistic behavior contained
It's even worse to attempt to point fingers at the culprit
I can't keep that feeling out of my skin, off my shirt to fix what has stained

I take to my knees at
the altar and bury
my face at the foot
of the pulpit

Forever my mind
dies, stuck almost as
if fried
I can face you
wholeheartedly and
tell you stories,
you'll never know I
lied...

War Wounds

*I have scars, I don't talk about them but they're there, Permanently, have you noticed them?
Can you read between the lines that are there?
Are you focusing? And what does my life mean to you?
Am I worth more than a few weeks of grieving?
Will you forget about the sound of my voice soon?
Will my words evaporate only to be seen again?
When it rains from them... them being your eyes,
What will you choose to wipe them away with?
A shirt? A tissue? A handkerchief?
Your memories of me?
What will you remember me as?
Can I be more than a gravestone in a land plot of people whose legacies we don't know?
Where will mine stand amongst theirs?
Will I be happily remembered?
Or will my funeral be bare like embalmed bodies?
Are my kids to even have me buried?*

*Or will I go down in flames?
Placed into an interior design accessory?
Maybe my ashes will be in the ocean consumed by fish who mistake them as flakes?
Am I destined to correctly write my mistakes?
Or teeter between right and wrong to determine my fate?
Pendulums swing in my mind, consumed in the times where I had your skin magnified just under your eyes with droplets,
If I'm praying, will it stop me from being preyed upon?
Will I know my enemies or will I befriend them?
Will I be the one to give them the tools to deceive me and stop me from breathing?
Can I change their minds and alter my own final destination?
And if I die before I wake, what will be the lessons they can only learn after I meet my fate?*

Tired of Runnin'

I'm tired of runnin...
I said I'm tired of runnin,
my feet splintered with the planks they made slaves walk on before drowning them in masses,
It's not just my history it's my blood lines where no love lies,
In spaces where my great uncle's love lies in that mausoleum after 60 yrs. of marriage,
Knowing I couldn't maintain a few years of solid friendship,
I'm kin with the ppl that taunted me,
I was never bullied by outsiders it's the insiders that haunted me,
My nephew stays flossing he...always had better clothes than me,
I wonder if he has infant memories of his mother's struggle,
The fight to breathe through his father's arms,
The struggle in scuffles between him and I,
I'd rather lose my life then watch her endure abuse again,
I'm runnin from the bones loosened in my mother's jaws because some punk ass dude lost his cool,
I was young then, but I want his soul in exchange for her healed past,
Strapped with the last of my emotions I wrap it in a bandana and put it on a stick,
Folded in between the blues that rang through my grandfather's life,
Just don't try to follow me,
Runnin from those bottles of NyQuil that swallowed me,
The Prozac that consumed my dreams,
The nightmares where I died many times,
I'm dyin of thirst, my hunger is hurt,
but to get a grip on the ground I have to stop runnin first, before I....

Superman

Expectations trouble me because it's a pre-created thesis,
They expect me to pick up and complete with puzzle pieces,
So i'm always picture perfect,
They feast on my imperfections because THEY are imperfect,
It's easy to be deceived by your purpose if you only see what you want to,
As a result, you block other people's view and it's hard to see through to what I'm supposed to do,
I tried to oppose the blues but sometimes the song is so much sweeter,
Melody is much more on rhythm than my heartbeat is,
I want you to check to make sure that I have a pulse,
see? I'm human too,
But it doesn't seem when they get their first impression in order,
And if it's positive they expect you to get out the boat and walk on water,
Being around a child frequently doesn't make a man a perfect father,
Be precautious with your judgements,

Prophecies From My Heart

Not saying I think I'm a bad person
or father just feels like I have more
to prove,
People staking claims in my name as
best dad, but my kids are still
young,
We ain't had much we have had to
go through,
So, your compliments are better
suited if they say "starting off good
as a dad"
But these problems go past me
being a parent,
They stretch past the borders of
professionalism,
They plague every talent I possess
so if I don't perform well or have
slip ups I'm looked down upon,
They never see the stress that fills
my face,
Because once upon a taste we were
all the same flavor,
I mean we all started at the bottom
level,
some maybe more privileged than
others,
So, it's hard to keep focus when the
objective seems hopeless,
And I hope less would come my way,
but I see scattered storms on the
radar,
I keep my head up, because it's hard
to see anything good coming your
way if you're only gazing at the
ground,
I can only be Superman sometimes,
but mostly I'm Peter Parker,

I mean I keep getting mixed so Kent Clark or anybody that's the opposite of trouble starter only promotes partials of my whole,
This is me, a human being, and unfortunately my emotions can sometimes get in the way so it's tough not to walk all over them,
But they are there so I only ask that you take consideration and step over there if you're not going to care for them...

This Is Why I Write

This is why I write... because I absolutely love words,
like if I could marry words and be with them for the rest of my life I would,
It would be soooo good plus the impact that it makes are seismic earthquakes, shakes in groundbreaking fashion,
I write for the voiceless and you don't know me but if you did you would understand what it means to me,
literally the world because it helps cure my depression,
excuse me, my anxiety,
pardon me,
My bipolar dis-order of business was made personal to forefront my aggressions,
I form my expressions and it feels so expressive,
I can't help but to fall in love over and over like it's a constant rekindling of words, the sparking of an entendre, innuendos out ya venues
What more are we looking for?
Allow me to elaborate, expound upon, sound off and arouse the tongues of other lyricists to come full force,
I love phrases,
Metaphors formed rock solid granite I could use something else,
but writing is so stone cold and diamond tough but my melanin sands tone down to the brown shades, caving in hieroglyphics and is such a beauty to read,
see what I did there?
They're looking for their reprieve then write to relieve,
Sometimes I like to write for myself just to please,
The satisfaction factors into word actions that's verbs acting like why fashion it,

Sometimes you need it raw direct and in your face like that one coworker without the filter,
Or stealth like words with hidden meaning,
If I can take full advantage of the idea of speaking feelings,
Touching words like Braille feeling, this is that comfort food for the soul filling,
Meditation and re-centred writing has my soul healing,
Everything equally entered enticing equivocal etymology evicting in entirety,
I LOVE WORDS!!!!
But another reason why I write is to have something to myself,
A legacy that helps vault me into void spaces where I can just be,
Placated in the pasts and presents of people's trials and tribulations,
Sometimes it's easier for somebody to release their story through somebody else,
It creates a path to go down when life drives you crazy,
I started in my teenage years where everything negative equaled the end of the world,
So, in retrospect I was accustomed to apocalypse like x-men comics,
Now through my growth my poetry is word vomit because everything that comes out is nasty!
See? I threw that in there to show that all this writing strengthened my forearms so I'm just flexin ink from my veins,
Writing was the hugs that I didn't get in childhood, the love I didn't get from my wild hoods, The deadbeat dad that I was missing,

Prophecies From My Heart

The girl of my dreams that I imagined kissin,
the lost friends and relatives I was reminiscing,
and my mental illness that was dominated by
the world that made me feel submissive,
So, I write, because it's right when I write for
the right to have rights,
With this pen I draw wings and start to take
flight,
Poetry is life!
There's not much about it to not like and that in
itself,
is one of the many reasons that I write,
Plus, words cut deep, and I'm deep thought so
fire sticks above the clouds in the sky...
it's a match made in heaven...

Everything Is Made Up

When I was a child I lead with my imagination
Hoping to be a sponge to the leaky eyes that surrounded me
Unspoken words in family that created a hindrance of growth
So, we indulge in secrecy secretly plotting on each other's downfall
But as children we are young, not dumb so we know what's going on but can't say a damn thing for fear of being popped in the mouth
"that's grown folk business so stay the fuck out of it!"
So, you're telling me that I'm supposed to ignore mama's broken jaw?
...And still be cool with the person who did it?!?
She can't talk and is bed ridden while he gets a slap on the wrist
Gets clearance to slap another bitch so she can fear him, because apparently that's what it's like to be a man
Please me and appease me
Inhale and breathe me, but if you step out of line in my mind, it's okay for me to literally put yours besides you
Maybe somewhere deep down, that's what kept me from black women
Is knowing the males in my family had a fine lineage of degrading
Downgrading black women that maybe I didn't wanna be a part of it

Prophecies From My Heart

In my generation I didn't wanna be the start of it
Because the same men I'm lookin up to tellin me to man up
While they got all these black eyes seeping from their knuckles
Swollen cheeks tattooed with the lines in their palms
Imprints of necks fitting perfectly to the inside of forearms
Bruises shower from rough encounters
Then to make matters worse they stepped out on the same women they beat
As if the physical abuse wasn't enough they had to demoralize them down to nothing
So, I'm surrounded by these unhappy women who were trying to figure it out, and me?
If I spoke up because it angered me it was a *"stop being pussy!"*
Or the classic *"you'll understand when you get older"*.
We want black women to hold boulders at the same time we rock them to pebbles
Then walk across them as they disintegrate to gravel
Fire has to be somewhere between 1,100 -2,400 degrees to melt rocks
So naturally we turn up the heat assuring us that you **WILL NEVER** be fair-in-height unless cells see us
But even then, you **NEED** to stay loyal no matter what it is we did to get in this predicament, use the kids as dividends
*"How the **FUCK** you gon keep me away from my child?"*

"Maybe that little bastard ain't mine anyway!"
I mean If I can't be with you I ain't takin care of it,
My mind took a share of it
Glare as if our stares could lift you by the neck alone strangling the women without even touching them
We inject them with paralytic drugs so they can't **DO** anything but can feel **EVERYTHING**
This must change no matter the risk
Because if it doesn't, black women will become extinct
And at the hands of black men, they will completely cease to exist
And let's not begin to mention how we leave them in the corner closed like finished books
Because there was enough interest to skim the pages but not enough to make you want to read until the end
So, we cruising through the library trying to find something that's easy to read with just pictures
We don't need chapters because this is a man's world, so we roam freely
Then turn around and cut with the broken glass from our shattered reflections
I don't need you because if you won't suck and fuck then **She** will
And even if **SHE** don't, we can train your daughters by making them feel important
Sometimes they turn to their own daughters,
nieces
cousins
sisters

Prophecies From My Heart

But that's on the down low so there's no 12 play because handcuffs are oppression
Free the bros even though they fucked that girl into suicide against her will
Her gravestone will be unjustified because she went there willingly
Short shirts and skirts are welcoming, if it's pleasing to the eye then please me or die
Even writing this piece make me sick to my stomach
BLACK WOMAN...I need you
I love you
I'll protect you
You have in me the product of the environment that I never confined to I just learned from
Without asking me I vow to be here for you, with you, beside you
In return I hope you feel happy, loved, respected, important, valued, appreciated, wanted, needed and more importantly safe...

Poetry Tears

This poem doesn't deserve my tears
because I don't cry anyway
they say you need to
which makes me retreat even further the
burdens of having your voice murdered
or at least flat lined for a little while
served up what we deserved but who's to
say what that really means
validation these days manifests as false
absolution via peers
so, I turn words to water and cry tears in
puddles that turns to poems, so my eyes
physically stay dry
can't get rid of me I don't die I live
through the tears the rain
the puddles
these letters those words, its water
overflowed these poems
when they ask me to recite something
they're asking me to cry and it's okay
because it's a cathartic type of cleanse
wash away my sins
hold on to my faith in God but wash away
the Christian

Prophecies From My Heart

I'm the anomaly they're not accepting me
to be what I wanna be and honestly that's
okay
I'm nobody's property polishing up my
emotions, so they look pretty
even though they're antiques because
they been around for a while
and I can't sell them for much but they're
of great value to me
in great volume you'd see the crack
where they leak
drip, drip, drip now we're back to the
water metaphors and concepts I'm woke
but unconscious I know what's
happening but can't do anything
unless I need to reproduce the effects of
divine intervention, poetic provisions
deceptive in a pro's vision
my poetry tears produce words to kill so
we can all experience and die in my
lyricism…period grammar screaming into
our ears
but these feelings need to breathe bitch
so step back to receive this
because if I hit you from the inside out
it'll cause your skin to start peeling

but then maybe we will be on even ground
because that's where we share resemblance
learn to harness the power of tears
the effect it has on your body the means of
expressing what's in your psyche so cry me
river meaning write poems that I can
drown in and for you I'll do the same
we can both die immortal because rivers
won't run dry, but the land can be
oversaturated in mental illness
meaning everybody in poetry got
something going on its ourselves meeting
up with ourselves and keeping us busy
do you understand what's going on
listening to my heartbeat but not the lyrics
of the song
and maybe my fingers don't make sounds
to click because I snap different, poetry
tears cried different
the passion and hopes of a single mother
within him
paved way for my poetry tears to
moisturize the dry grounds to provide a
softer side to women

Prophecies From My Heart

I was born a love child and as a child I
thought that was a means to
romanticism but now I realize it's the
actions that correspond with a vision
in those sight lines I acknowledge that
if woman is maybe a rib because it's
connected to our spine and over our
hearts
but what shields the protection from
what tries to make them yield
these poetry tears will form a force
field, so you won't go down alone, so
cry with me love, cry...

A New Faith

I've seen the breath escape from my brethren
the other day
blood leaked out his veins and inked in some
stains that resembled a crucifix
Lucifer mixed with his demons breeding off
the killings between heathens
and the bodies of the sinners at their funerals
when deceased then...
I closed my eyes to pray for a new faith,
placed promptly in the middle of trials and
tribulations
I contribute to the debate that drama follows
me
I bottled my emotions and let it all just
swallow me
but through the mouth of that bottle, I saw
light
so, it's a given that I change my stroke and
start swimmin
I mean change my stroke so it's different
when I'm hittin birdies like I'm throwing
doves
like my life is conflicted but still centred on
love
I made a come up from pharmaceutical drugs
and wrist cuts into the body of Christ and
being baptized in his blood
now smiles put me in the predicament to
wonder if He's real

Prophecies From My Heart

*His blessings are naturally heaven sent and
His powers are infinite, miracles are his
will
we make it out the dark when we decide to
repent our sins so he can reveal that in
time all wounds will heal
a new faith lets me know that He's there
my animalistic behavior didn't make me
strong but now tame, I know that I can
bear
anything that decides to mount my
shoulders and as I get older, I know that
He walks with me
talks with me, and assures me that my
belief in Him will be redeemed
when my spirit ascends but until then let it
be known that you're a child of God and
never be ashamed or hold it within
He wouldn't be afraid to claim you as His
to share with you all He has down to the
communion of his blood and body
He was reincarnated into the Holy Spirit,
so opaque, so there
so, refreshing like this new faith has left
me without any extremities to count up all
my blessings
and if you see that cross realize it's not a
symbol but it's sacred of the place where
He gave his life for us to live*

the spikes burrowed into His healing hands
driven through the feet He walked on water with
the crown of thorns that pierced into His temples but never touched the faith of His churches
I was looking for a new faith, now this faith is embraced and set me on a path to reach the eternal just beyond the heavenly gates
where God will welcome me with open arms and say "my child I've been waiting for you
come live with me and be of eternal blessings" and I'll bask in my new faith until that day
in the name of the Father, the Son and the Holy Spirit
let us all say...

My 1st Birthday

I have this picture of myself as a baby
and I'm holding on to this stuffed
blue bunny
I don't know where it came from or if
I had ever given it a name
I still have it 30+ years later
I was born on August 1st. 1988
it was a day of firsts, first second,
minute, hour, day on this earth
first time meeting my mother and the
fourth time she gave birth
I was a c-section baby, so my mother
was cut open and I was pulled out of
the world I knew into this one
1st bath that day, first meal outside
an umbilical cord
hell backtracking...it was the first day
of that month
my mom was born January 1st, so I
guess there was some correlation
She was fairly religious
not beat you with rulers and
memorizing verses religious but
vacation Bible school
Wednesday night Bible study
Sunday morning bible study then
service
children's and mass choir type of
religious

John 11:35 *Jesus wept* it's the shortest
verse in the Bible but I mean what else
needs to be said,
even the words in red couldn't change
what you read when those words ease into
your spirit
Mama cried too, a lot, she wasn't Jesus, but
she loved the same
compresses. composed, potent of estrogen
and toxic emotions release suppressed
pain translated to our stairwell wall
covered in perfume stains
the glass was the fragility of her heart, the
smell was the beauty of it
the first time I thought my mother was
crazy
back in my suicidal days she forced fed me
advice, prayer, gospel
and people who told me a friend of mine
was going to hell because he committed
suicide
I was surrounded by blunt objects
they just weren't effective, one night
became the first night I slapped my mother
with the word bitch and made sure it cut
deep
I left and for the first time felt like dying
was my best option to find peace
the first time I really felt abandonment in
what was supposed to be my home
I have the ability to not feel physical pain
and so I never flinched from the razor
blades just waited for the blood to run to
see if I was still of this world

Prophecies From My Heart

I was...*Jesus wept,*
two words and in the world of poets,
words hold more power than anything
what terrifies you?
And what happens when you have to face that fear?
After I watched my mother die, I screamed
I'm not sure how loud but it's the first time my worst fears came true,
that's the first time I would walk out of that hospital for the last time
the first time everything wouldn't be okay
the first time I had to accept you weren't here to stay
the first time something made me numb to the point where I wasn't feeling mental or emotional pain
so, I don't know how many times I got hit with those razor blades, but I knew
they'd come back, and steel sharpens steel
still chafing until they cut through but this time, I didn't see blood just mama's tears
so, does this mean I am no longer of this world?
Because I don't have blood anymore just bloodletting sacrificing the filters she kept on me,
the lessons she instilled **the feel, the feel, THE FEEL!**

the fact that I would kill to hear you
and wanted you there to help me
through this
but the selfishness of my isolation
placed me promptly on top of
trophies
to be proud to stand in your golden
embrace and this poem is about my
first birthday
my first birthday without you
where nobody sings to me in your
voice, nobody takes me out to eat
nobody smiles that big cheesy ass
smile you gave me
and nobody posts a collage of my life
on their Facebook
where frankly fuck them but it still
felt good
my first birthday is the last first
birthday without you
and the first time I accepted that I'm
not of this world…nor do I have to
be…

Prophecies From My Heart

The depth of my thoughts is entirely dependent on your pain tolerance,
Mine has skyrocketed over the years,
so much so that many of my poems mention my tears,
And it's ironic because I don't cry much outside of tragedy,
It's not a choice or numbness just the normalization of my reality,
My heart chose to speak throughout these processes
Prophecies are predictions and predictions are forecasts of things to come,
Believe it or not when I was a child, I spoke little...I was preparing mentally
I was becoming aware that life would be difficult once I opened up
I trained myself not to feel physical pain unless I wanted to
I wasn't aware that the process would force me to do the same mentally
So, my pain tolerance skyrocketed beyond my own comprehension
It's like urinary retention, I could hold it in until it was forced out of me

*So, the prophecies of my heart were often out of context
Couldn't perceive the contents of my conscience displayed bare naked
When I was in high school being open nearly killed me
I trusted everybody and held on to the belief that popularity was everything
My world was changed by one of the most beautiful girls I ever laid eyes on
She showed me the world was real, She showed me that death was real, and pain was inevitable
She was the reason and beginning of my poetry running deep
Sticks and stones may break bones, but my words nearly killed us both
You overdosed on pills and had to go to the hospital
I felt sick to my stomach, I felt responsible for everything
I had to find a way to cope with that grief
I tried to cut through the layers of my skin hoping to reach an artery
I kept cutting trying to find the piece of life where things got better
But the only thing that came out of me was blood,*

Prophecies From My Heart

*I was disappointed that mine was
normal because I didn't feel
normal
I felt like my heart and soul
paralleled my pain
That was different but maybe
that's just life through my
opinion
I believe I am a poetic prophet so
from my heart came these
prophecies
And in the depth of those
prophecies is the eye of my
mother's legacy
And since neither of us could
breathe forever
I forced my lungs on to paper
because those words can
And at this point you should've
felt them breathe
Sync with them and stay close as
you continue to take this walk
with me
To be continued...*

www.ingramcontent.com/pod-product-compliance
Lightning Source LLC
Chambersburg PA
CBHW072201160426
43197CB00012B/2476